Orange Roses:

A Memoir on Mental Health from One Family's Perspective

By Krista Fliger, Katie Mast, and Ivan Mast Jr

Edited by Matthew Caracciolo

Cover illustrations by Sevgi Master

Published by Krista Fliger, Ivan Mast, and Katie Mast. May 2023. Kindle Direct Publishing.

ISBN: 9798394016059

I dedicate this book to my sweet son, London Carter, loyal husband Clint, and to anyone who has ever lived with a mental illness. There is hope of living a joy-filled and meaningful life despite any diagnosis you may face.

~Krista

"I was never really insane except upon occasions when my heart was touched."

-Edgar Allan Poe

"Why did you do all this for me?' He asked. 'I don't deserve it. I've never done anything for you.' 'You have been my friend," replied Charlotte. "That in itself is a tremendous thing.'"

E.B. White, Charlotte's Web

"People are often unreasonable and self-centered. Forgive them anyway. If you are kind people may accuse you of ulterior motives. Be kind anyway. If you are honest, people may cheat you. Be honest anyway." Mother Teresa

Acknowledgments

Krista

I am writing this book for you. You who are somewhere in the dark and cannot see the way out. You who have lost your sense of direction, and are perhaps struggling with mental illness for the first time or the 300th. I'm writing my story to inspire someone else to not give up and to have hope, to know that there can be some semblance of normalcy again.

I'd like to first give glory to God, the Trinity, for allowing me to go through all this in order to make his name known and to help others. I prayed for Him to use me and he has.

Secondly, my husband for being there by my side through thick and thin. And my amazing son for being the sweetest person I know and for being my cheerleader.

My best friends Steffi Smith, Michelle Wilkinson, and Rachel Jackson for sticking "closer than a (sister)" and bringing me orange roses and hope always.

My church and Pastors for ministering to my heart so I could pour into others.

All my teachers and professors through the years, with special thanks to the Cedarville University Psychology professors and Ashland Theological Seminary professors who taught me to "find my voice" and the basics of how to handle my thoughts.

My counselor Honor Worthington, who saw something in my story and me, nudged me to write down thoughts from my experience, and proposed that maybe I could write a book from them to help others! Without her, this book would not exist! Thanks for believing in me and being a servant of Christ.

All the people who have poured into me over the years, too many to count, leading me closer to Jesus and toward counseling school.

Thanks Jeff Beachy for editing our rough draft. Thanks to my friends Matthew Caracciolo and Sevgi Master, for, in this order, finding our typos and making beautiful illustrations for our cover. Thanks to Sheri Hooley for her help in self publishing on Kindle Direct Publishing! We are forever grateful to all of you.

And finally but not least of all, my parents, who raised me and still love me unconditionally as their daughter and who never gave up on me. Thanks for telling your side of the story through this book (Ivan II and Katie Mast).

Contents

Chapter 1…Childhood for Krista 1

Chapter 2…The Tsunami 7

Chapter 3…The Airport 15

Chapter 4…The First Hospitalization 21

Chapter 5…Angels 27

Chapter 6…Coming to Terms 31

Chapter 7…The Good Times 35

Chapter 8…The Summer Breakdown 39

Chapter 9…The Outer Banks Crisis 45

Chapter 10…A Miracle 49

Chapter 11…The Wrong Place 53

Chapter 12…Bible Characters and Cigarettes 59

Chapter 13…Unraveling 61

Chapter 14…The Third Hospitalization 67

Chapter 15...The Diagnosis   73

Chapter 16...A Lucky One   79

Chapter 17...What Has Helped Me   83

Chapter 18...NIMH Study   89

Chapter 19...What I've Learned   93

Chapter 20...It Takes All of Us   97

Chapter 21...This Present Moment   105

Chapter 1

Childhood For Krista

Ivan

I was twenty-seven years old when I became a father. I was more ready than not when Krista Danielle Mast burst into our lives that May day in 1988. She was a tiny, beautiful baby and my wife Katie and I were thrilled with the new addition to our family.

Krista was a happy, kind and content child. She was always comfortable around us but very shy around strangers. She started saying some words around a year old and started singing songs around the house soon after that. Krista was a bright child and was able to learn things easily.

Wherever we went with Krista she received, much to her chagrin, a tremendous amount of attention due to her Shirley Temple hair and clear blue eyes. When she was two and a half years old, her brother Ivan III was born. Krista immediately adored her brother, holding him with our help.

Around four years old Krista started having night terrors in the early part of her sleep cycle. She would appear to be awake while crying inconsolably. Sometimes rocking her would get her sleeping peacefully again. Other times a car ride would do the trick; occasionally we found laying her in a secure basket on top of the running dryer and then placing her back into her bed took away her terrors. As she got a bit older, the night terrors stopped.

Disciplining Krista was hardly ever needed, but I do remember one time I made the mistake of swatting her behind and it broke her heart as well as mine. I never swatted her again. Her tender and kind spirit was constantly on display.

Although Krista was shy, she was an adventurous spirit who talked us into sending her on a "People to People" trip to Hawaii. We encouraged her to play sports and participate in other activities and she became good at soccer, playing through high school and during her freshman year in college.

Krista was a parent's dream child, a good student who was never in trouble. She was inducted into the National Honor Society, was named co-captain of her soccer team and was voted homecoming queen by her high school peers. Krista knew no enemies nor did she threaten anyone in return; she was kind and considerate to everyone.

After high school Krista decided to forgo college for a year and joined Adventure In Missions, choosing England as her assignment. It was hard for me to see my daughter leave and I cried all the way to the airport and for a number of days thereafter. Katie would laugh when I would say "the missionaries stole my baby".

Katie and I traveled to Salford, England to visit Krista during her gap year, and I now recognize what might have been the first signs that Krista would later deal with mental illness. In England, something as subtle as the different colors she saw at dinner might have significance in telling her what choices she should make. While I thought this odd,

I gave it just a fleeting thought, but with hindsight it now seems clear.

After finishing her assignment in England, Krista decided to attend a small college in northern Georgia. She completed her freshman year in Georgia and then transferred to a sister school not far from New York City. Near the end of her junior year, Krista had difficulty sleeping and felt some scary thoughts while living in her apartment, sensing an evil presence around her. We later discovered that Krista struggled far more than we realized. We were clueless.

When she came home for Christmas, Krista was definitely not herself, crying and experiencing anguish in ways that I had never before seen in her. I didn't know what to say or do to comfort her and remember breaking down in despair more than once. Little did we know a tsunami was building that would hit us with a force we could not have imagined.

Chapter 2

The Tsunami

Ivan

When I dropped Krista off at the airport on a cold early January day, I knew something was off. She had signed up to go to Israel with some professors and students from her college and was ready to leave that morning. Before she went through security she came back to where I was standing and said "Dad, this guy in front of me is really weird" and was talking about wanting to get away from him.

I was perplexed and worried as I left, but Krista assured me that she was okay and proceeded through security. As I was driving back from the airport that morning, I received a call from Krista and I realized that Krista was struggling. After boarding her plane, Krista became very paranoid and ran off the plane and back into the airport. I was shocked, as I know how difficult it is to leave a boarded plane. By the time I got back to the airport, the airline had pulled her luggage from the plane and she was waiting for me.

She hurriedly told me that there were evil people on the plane and was talking anxiously about why she needed to get off the flight. My mind and heart rate were racing as we drove back to meet Katie and her brother for lunch. I was trying to stay calm, but inside I was a mess. As the day progressed, Krista started becoming scared even of us; towards evening, her thoughts were becoming delusional.

Krista didn't feel she needed help, insisting that she was fine. We hoped, naively, that she would be okay after a good night's sleep. We tried getting her to go upstairs to her room to lie down and try to sleep. Krista was nowhere near being able to fall asleep, we just didn't know that yet. We were just starting to realize how difficult it might be to get her help.

As the night wore on Krista became more agitated, scared, paranoid and delusional. Our goal became to keep her safe until morning and then seek help. The rest of the night was a blur as Katie and I tried to figure out how to survive the night. I gave Krista a Benadryl which proved to be like trying to stop a gaping wound with a Band-Aid. She told us later that she thought I had given her cocaine, which caused her to become suspicious of everything we said and did.

Sometime in the early morning hours, Krista became extremely restless. She began pacing and wanted to leave the house. Katie was upstairs trying to calm her and I was laying at the bottom of the steps to prevent her from running out into the frigid winter night. I left the stairway unprotected for a brief moment and Krista ran downstairs and bolted out the front door into the cold snow and darkness before we could react. Krista was barefoot while I was in my socks. I dashed for my shoes and, after what seemed like an eternity, went outside not knowing in which direction Krista had fled. I felt fear like I had never before known.

The ground was frozen but without enough snow to see tracks, so I began blindly running into the darkness and bitter cold, my adrenaline surging. I knew I needed to find Krista quickly before she suffered from exposure. My senses were on hyper alert as I ran, frantic to find her. I somehow stumbled upon her two houses down the road from our house, huddled under an evergreen tree. As I neared her, she bolted away again as if she feared for her life, running through the trees towards our house. Exhausted, she finally slowed down enough for me to catch up with her on a steep bank behind our wooded property. She shrieked as I tried to comfort her and calm her down but it was useless. In her delusional mind, she felt sure I was planning to kill her.

I tried to lift her tiny body of barely 100 pounds and carry her back to the warmth of our home, but I was too exhausted to lift her as she frantically struggled to free herself. I screamed into the night for help. Katie was outside by now and heard me. I asked her to go in and get her brother to help me, as it was all I could do to keep her from breaking free.

Her brother quickly came out and thankfully she simply let him lift her and carry her back into the house. I was very thankful that her brother Ivan had been home from college for Christmas break and was there to help in this critical moment. I have always marveled at how her brother remains calm through times like these.

The rest of the night Ivan, Katie and I lay in front of each exit door on the main floor to prevent Krista from escaping again. At daybreak, I called my brother, an ER doctor, and asked him to come over and help us figure out what to do next. While he rushed over, he called a local hospital and prepared them for our arrival. Getting her into the car was a struggle, but we finally managed. Luckily, we had safety locks and could prevent Krista from opening the doors while driving to the hospital.

We were admitted quickly to the hospital where drug and alcohol tests were done. After several hours, we found a mental health facility about a half-hour drive away. Krista received an injection to calm her down so that we were able to drive her to the mental health facility. Only later would we realize how difficult it can be to get into an ER and to find a mental health facility accepting patients

without a long delay.

Chapter 3

The Airport

Krista Fliger

I never imagined that I was heading toward a trip to a mental hospital. It started on a trip with my father to our local airport. The small Christian college I was attending in New York offered a Biblical Holy Lands class in Israel which would begin right after the Christmas and New Year's holidays. I signed up for the class before heading home for the holiday break. My college boyfriend and I had just broken up and my sadness from that, combined with the short days surrounding the winter solstice, added gloom to the holidays. I felt off, a little detached from my family and even from myself.

Christmas and New Year's passed and soon it was nearly time to go to the airport to travel to Israel. I had trouble preparing for my trip, finding it difficult to pack my suitcase with the items I would need. On the way to the airport, my dad and I talked about how I thought America was under attack. My dad didn't say much about it, but probably thought I had some weird political views.

My dad and I walked to the concourse and, after a hug goodbye, I got in line to go through security. I sensed that the person behind me was crying. I said "I'm going to Israel" to her and I thought she said "I know." This scared me and I moved farther back in line. Things were starting to get blurry around me. Somehow, I made it to my gate and boarded my flight to New York, where I'd meet up with my classmates and teacher before we would all head to Israel together.

I made it through security and onto the plane. From my seat, I noticed a man across the aisle. For some reason I noticed his braces and I said "I like your braces" and he said "thanks, I did them myself." This frightened me, and I grabbed my bag and ran off the plane. Fortunately, no one stopped me and I was able to get back to the concourse.

My thinking continued to be blurry, but I managed to call my dad and asked him to come back and pick me up. I must have looked lost, because a police officer came over to me and asked where I was going. He looked at my phone. I told him my dad was coming to pick me up. After he gave my phone back, he let me go. I had been talking to myself which is probably why the officer questioned me. Thankfully I had a good experience with law enforcement. Looking back, I realize it could have gone a lot worse.

While waiting for my father to return, I walked into an airport shop. I remember thinking Santa Claus was bad for stealing the attention from Jesus on Christmas, so I knocked over a few Santa dolls on display. A stranger picked them up and looked at me strangely.

Finally, my dad drove up and I got in the car with him. We met my brother and mom at Chipotle for lunch. My parents are excellent at knowing how to make me comfortable, but this time their help was not enough to keep me sane.

When I got home, I was trying to contact my professor so I could still go on the trip, but my mom said to just let it go. Since she wouldn't let me contact my professor, I drove to a friend's house. I was still in a blurry thinking mode, but I was doing my best to contact my professor, thinking that my mom was holding me back. My friend's parents were kind to me. I'm not sure if they knew anything was wrong with me at this point. Finally, I drove home after not being able to contact my professor in my confused state.

The rest of the day is a blur, but it ended with me sitting in the snow looking up at the moon. I started thinking that Jesus was coming back that night and I had to be outside waiting for him. My mom finally got me inside and stayed up with me all night. I apparently wanted to pray all night. In the morning, my parents called my uncle, a doctor, to come over and help take me to the hospital. I remember being scared of my own family, and what they might do to me even though they'd never hurt me in my life.

I ran through the yard to get away, wondering if there was any house I could run to. My dad and my brother were chasing me in the snow. My mom said she remembers me being barefoot, a detail I had forgotten but makes me shudder now. Finally, my brother brought me inside the house. They got me into the car and took me to a nearby emergency room. There they gave me a shot and I signed consent papers to be admitted into a nearby mental hospital.

Chapter 4

The First Hospitalization

Katie

I was getting frustrated. Krista was on Christmas break from college, and was supposed to be packing to leave for a school trip to Israel the next morning. Instead, she was on the floor in her room with a blank look and an empty suitcase. Hardly masking my exasperation, I told her, "It's not that hard. You look at the list, and then you put those things in your suitcase."

I had no idea what Krista was going through at the time. We knew she was struggling, but it's not unusual for young adults to struggle. Krista had successfully navigated through the challenges of childhood and adolescence, and I had no reason to doubt her ability to overcome the difficulties of this life stage as well.

By the following day, however, I knew something was very wrong. Krista reported that people around her at the airport and on the airplane were acting very weird. She was scared and got off the plane before it left the gate. It was a huge relief that she did. The flight was bound for New York's JFK airport, not a good place for a person who is alone, confused and frightened.

Krista's behavior deteriorated throughout the day. Her mind seemed to be racing out of control. That night she talked and prayed, talked and prayed, but did not sleep. We began to fear for her actual safety as she became suspicious and afraid of us.

She ran from us into the dark, frigid night. After we caught up with her, we had to physically carry her inside and later into the car and to the hospital.

While it was distressing to us, it was also a relief when the next morning we got Krista to an inpatient psychiatric facility where she would receive treatment and be kept safe. Her father and I visited as soon as we were allowed. She didn't speak and showed no recognition of us. I remember stroking her hair and talking to her. We bought Dr. Pepper, her favorite drink. We also brought a few photos, which I later found torn up in pieces in the trash. She was locked away somewhere out of our reach.

Over the next few days, Krista remained non-verbal on our visits but began to wander about restlessly. One afternoon, I received a call from the facility.

The voice on the other end reported that Krista had gone out of an opened door and they currently did not know her whereabouts. The police were searching for her.

Wait. What? This was a secure unit. For us to visit, we had to enter through two locked doors. On this day, the director had come into the unit through a side door, and Krista was there when the door opened and immediately slipped out. She ran down the stairwell and out into the chill air, barefoot and wearing only capris and a t-shirt.

The security department of a local college found Krista knocking on the door of a residence. She was handcuffed, given a shot, and taken back to her unit, where she was somewhat of a local hero to the rest of the patients for successfully "escaping."

When Krista was a safety threat to herself or others, she was involuntarily medicated, but as she improved and was no longer considered a threat, she could decline her medication, something she often did, typically with a polite, "no, thank you." One night as visiting hours were ending, and Krista once again refused her medication, my husband, in desperation, pleaded with the nurse to keep trying. The nurse told us she planned to try again later that evening, but if we waited a moment she would attempt again now. We waited. She came back and told us she had succeeded, and we drove home, at least that time, much relieved. Such extra effort by nurses and hospital staff meant much to us.

Krista's first hospitalization lasted eight days. On about day seven, she began clearing, as if heavy clouds were finally lifting. She became more like herself than she'd been in a long time. It was an amazing and deeply joyous experience for us. She described it as feeling like someone hit a reset button.

We had a lot of questions. What does this mean? Why did it happen, and will it happen again? Krista's doctor was compassionate and encouraging. It was too soon to know a lot of the answers, but I remember him assuring her and us that she would still be able to pursue a career, get married and have a family. We recalled those words many times, because they gave all of us a lot of hope. There was much we had to learn.

Chapter 5

Angels

Krista

I hazily remember some of my time in the hospital, but large blocks are a complete blank. I remember thinking the people working in the hospital were evil, and that I was in a scary place. My parents would bring me Dr Pepper, which they knew was my favorite soda, and that was the only sense of reality I had. They visited me every chance they could. I became friends with others in the hospital. One lady called me an angel and another told me stories of a visiting guardian angel. Another woman held her arms out like a bird. I knew this was weird, even while being "out of it." My first roommate had been in some fights and was a little rough, so my dad requested a new roommate for me. The new roommate had been a victim of domestic violence and was very nice and left me alone.

The nurses would come in with my medicine and offer it to me. At first I didn't trust them and would say "no, thank you." Since I was an adult patient, all they could do was try to convince me to take it. I give a lot of credit to the hospital staff.

One day, I was standing near the entrance door. When an employee opened the door, I dashed outside. I was barefoot and there was snow on the ground, but I thought I was escaping somewhere bad and had to get to a house for help. After running around for a time, the staff found me and took me back in handcuffs. My mom said they gave me a shot. I don't remember what happened after that. My dad later told me that I was the only one the staff ever knew of that escaped the hospital, which gave us a laugh.

Fortunately for me, a doctor in my hospital knew the medicine I needed and how to effectively treat my condition. That doctor would become instrumental in my healing. The nurses learned to know me and how to get me to take my medicine. When I accepted the medicine, I started feeling better. One day I noticed that the television in the common room was tuned to a football game; and I remember watching it and thinking "Oh, yeah, football...real life." I was starting to come back to reality.

My doctor didn't offer me or my family a diagnosis while I was in the hospital, nor for some time after I was released; this would prove to be wise. Not having a diagnosis to fret over helped me find the courage to go back to school, finish my bachelor's degree in psychology, acquire my master's degree in counseling, get married, and have a beautiful child. But more on that later!

Chapter 6

Coming to Terms

Krista

After I left the hospital, I transferred from my New York college to another Christian college closer to my home. I was older than most of the students, which, combined with my shyness, made it harder for me to make new friends. I was also missing the friends I left behind at my previous college. Despite these challenges, things were going pretty well. I enjoyed my psychology and Bible classes.

I got along with my new roommate and the girls on my floor. I also started dating a guy I'll call Alex. He was younger than me, and I met him at a swing dancing night at the college where he was one of the instructors. He was a good dancer. The girls in my dorm and the guys in my "brother dorm" were trying to get us to date, so I said yes.

I had no experience with mental illness besides my one breakdown. Since things were going well and also because I didn't know better, I kept lowering my medicine dosage until I was down to basically nothing by the end of fall.

That winter, my mind started to unravel again. By the end of the semester, I was sure my professors were talking about me. At times I thought I had already died. Other times I thought that I was experiencing the end of the world. I remember seeing salt chunks spread on the winter roads and thinking they were diamonds. My boyfriend Alex was a huge help to me during my confused state.

One night he drove me home (about a forty minute drive) because I was so "out of it."

This was when I learned I still needed my medicine. I was coming to terms with the fact that what I was experiencing might actually be a disease and not a one-time incident. Part of mental illness is thinking you don't need medicine. Learning that, indeed, you do need to take medication can be a crucial step in getting healthy.

I managed to avoid going to the hospital that time, but for the next semester, I remained at home, commuting to college rather than living in the dorm. Alex and I broke up, which was yet another heartbreak.

Chapter 7

The Good Times

Krista

In college, I studied psychology with a counseling track. My professors advised me that I would need to earn a master's degree if I wanted to become a counselor. My program required that I complete an internship; I did mine at a counseling center, answering phones and connecting clients with counselors. I was given some good leads for counseling work from my internship, but first I was off to New Orleans.

In the spring of 2012, I started dating my now husband, Clint, who was a friend from my freshman year in college. After graduating with my bachelor's degree in counseling, I moved to New Orleans to be closer to Clint, where I lived in a house with two other women. Clint proposed to me soon after I moved to New Orleans. I was overjoyed and started planning our wedding. We went to premarital counseling in New Orleans at a Christian counseling center.

We had to decide if we would remain in New Orleans or move to Ohio to be closer to my parents. We visited New Orleans Baptist Theological Seminary and I checked out their counseling program. We had to take my health into consideration and the help we would get from my parents if we moved home. The cost of living was also significantly lower in Ohio, so after weighing our options, we decided to move north. Back in

Ohio, I applied to Ashland Theological Seminary, one of the schools recommended to me during my internship. I was ecstatic to learn that I had been accepted!

Clint and I married in August on a warm and sunny day. We had a wonderful wedding, and afterwards drove to Montreal for our honeymoon. We were happy to be together and optimistic about our future. After returning from the honeymoon, I babysat for a year then I started graduate school. Over the next two and a half years, I studied counseling theories and learned applied skills. I also completed another counseling internship, where I counseled and made a difference in the lives of others who, like me, struggled with mental health. It was rewarding work. I graduated in May

2017 with my Masters in Clinical Mental Health Counseling. While coping with the daily struggles of mental illness, I was able to get married and earn my master's. God blessed me and carried me through, but not before another mental health crisis.

Chapter 8

The Summer Breakdown

Katie

This wasn't how our extended family beach vacation was supposed to go. Krista was having trouble sleeping. She thought she was dying or had died. One day, she told me the people on the fishing pier were disciples of Jesus from the Bible. It was clear she needed to go home.

Krista had been stable for years. She was now happily married, in graduate school, and doing well. She and her husband made the decision to taper off her medication for the summer. The symptoms of mental illness were steadily returning.

We decided my mother, Krista, and I would leave vacation early. It was about a five-hour drive from the beach to the retirement center where mom was living, and another seven hours home. That night at my mom's place, I stayed in the same room with Krista to keep her from wandering out. The next day Krista and I left for home. I was terrified that she would break away from me, and as I drove I ran scenarios through my mind of what to do if she did. After something to eat at a fast food stop, I suggested we use the restroom. She said she didn't need to go and would wait for me in the restaurant. I asked her to go with me. She refused, so I just got back in the car.

Krista began taking medication again when she got home, but the effect was far from immediate. Three days later, she and her husband were visiting us at our rural home. Without speaking, Krista walked from the deck down the steps into our backyard, her dog at her heels. We called her, but she didn't turn around. Instead, she began to run. We scrambled after her, but she had a head start. The sound of barking led us to the dog, who was inside the next-door neighbor's garage. Krista was nowhere in sight.

What followed was hours of searching. Neighbors, friends, and family members came out in full force. The police, firemen, and EMTs arrived. Everyone was combing the area and calling her name. It began to get dark. I couldn't imagine where she could be. The police had checked with all the neighbors. The outbuildings had been searched, as had the woods behind our house. A search helicopter came and went. Our pastor invited people to gather on our driveway. We formed a circle and held hands while some prayed out loud. It was a beautiful moment of community.

As darkness set in, I heard the whir of another helicopter. The police told us this one had infrared capabilities and I felt hopeful as it circled low, searching the area. Perhaps she was lost in one of the cornfields. Finally, it turned, lifted and headed away. My hopes sank.

Eventually, the search was suspended until daybreak. I couldn't go inside the house. Our son helped me pull a piece of furniture from the deck onto the driveway, and I found a blanket. Just as the emergency responders began pulling out, I noticed movement coming from the other end of the road. I saw a familiar shape, walking my way, and I began running. Krista!

For hours, we had worried that Krista was huddled in the woods somewhere, wet and frightened. Or, even more disturbing, that she had somehow been swept into the swollen creek in our backyard. Instead, she was warm and dry and wondering what all the excitement was about. She was wearing a sweater that wasn't hers. Where did that come from, and where had she been?

From the next-door neighbor's house, Krista had crossed the road to another house and, without the knowledge of the owners, slipped down the stairs into a finished basement room. These neighbors later told us they found their books, furniture, and candles in an elaborate arrangement. Native American artwork had been removed from the walls, and some of it was torn up. The sweater Krista was wearing belonged to the woman. All of this could've elicited an angry response from our neighbors, or worse, but these understanding people extended nothing but complete kindness to us and to Krista.

Chapter 9

The Outer Banks Crisis

Krista

During the summer of 2015, after my first year of graduate school, I stopped taking my medicine because Clint and I decided that I would try to get pregnant. For a few months everything went okay, but I found myself crying more often than before. In July, I went to the Outer Banks to vacation with my mother's side of the family, something we did annually when I was young, either in the Outer Banks or in Virginia near the home of my maternal grandmother. I've always loved the beach and ocean, likely because of these reunions. Clint remained at home due to work.

Early in the vacation, I was moody and had trouble sleeping. I began to imagine that Jesus was returning. When my mental condition became noticeable, my mom left early to take me home. During the ride home, I thought that I had died. I made it home, but my condition deteriorated. Clint and my parents were trying to keep me out of the hospital by encouraging me to get back on my medication. One evening, Clint and my family were all playing kickball outside my parents' home. All of a sudden, I thought I was supposed to look for someone. Jesus? My soulmate? I wasn't sure, but in the middle of the game, I suddenly ran off into the surrounding woods.

My parents used to live in a nearby house and I ran there first. The door was locked, so I ran to a neighbor's house across the street. Here I found an unlocked door, and went down to the basement and stayed there for hours.

Eventually, I walked upstairs and discovered it was dark outside. I saw flashing lights from a fire truck; I was unaware that emergency personnel, along with my family and neighbors, were searching for me. I left the house and walked towards the lights, thinking it was a sign that Jesus had finally returned. The emergency personnel found me and took me to the hospital, where after an examination I was diagnosed with bipolar I disorder. I was given some warm socks (once again I had run off barefooted!) along with information on my diagnosis, and was allowed to leave with my husband and parents. Soon after leaving the hospital my medicine kicked in.

My mom helped me get back on my feet after this episode. We were wondering if I would be ready to go back to school in the fall. Somehow, miraculously, I was ready right before school started and was able to complete the semester while maintaining a good grade average.

Chapter 10

A Miracle

Krista

I graduated in 2017 with my Masters in Clinical Mental Health Counseling. After graduation, I wanted to look for a counseling job, but my husband and I agreed it would be best to wait due to the new medicines I would be taking. These medicines were safer for pregnancy, as Clint and I longed to have a baby of our own. We considered adopting and even surrogacy but neither option seemed completely right for us at the time for various reasons.

In the summer of 2017, I switched meds and, as I seemed to be doing fine, we stopped using birth control. The very next month I noticed that I had to go to the bathroom frequently. I purchased a pregnancy test and was amazed and delighted when it came back positive. We were in disbelief (especially Clint!) and he encouraged me to purchase additional tests, all of which also came back positive. We had not anticipated becoming pregnant so soon but were overjoyed.

The pregnancy went well. I was active with prenatal yoga and massages, I ate healthy and stopped drinking any alcohol. We read books and took parenting and birthing classes and watched each month as my belly grew in size. It was so much fun! When we found out that we would have a son, we were overjoyed, not because we preferred a specific gender, but from the joy of learning more about our baby. We decided on a name early on. Because of hormones released during pregnancy, many expectant women experience improved mental health. This was definitely true in my case. I had an easy pregnancy and gave birth to our son London on a rainy spring night. The first year with our son went by quickly and was very rewarding.

During that first year with London, I remained on medication that was better for pregnancy. I enjoyed being a new mom, but parenting certainly involves some stress and sleepless nights. I had also begun working as a counselor, and we had recently signed a contract for our first home. I was beginning to feel overwhelmed by the move we would soon make into a neighborhood. We celebrated our son's first birthday with our family, but as London was mashing his hands into the cake, my mental health was deteriorating. Without warning, I was back in the hospital, this time at a place we would end up calling the "wrong place."

Chapter 11

The Wrong Place

Ivan

In June, nearly ten years after Krista's first hospitalization, I began to sense another psychotic episode was nearing. Through the intervening years, she had been able to fight off several near misses by upping her medicine dosage, but this time would be different. What a helpless feeling for a father! Thankfully, the warm weather would mean that if she ran off again, at least she wouldn't be running barefoot through snow and ice.

Krista had gone on different medications to allow her to try and conceive, and to her, Clint and our delight she became pregnant. The pregnancy went better than any of us could have imagined and soon our grandson was born. One of Krista's doctors later explained that hormones released during pregnancy can protect mothers from psychiatric disorders and foster a period of emotional well-being, which is what I believe happened to Krista.

Less than a year after the birth of her son, Krista showed signs of becoming more ill with each passing week. I began to see a glaze in her beautiful blue eyes along with other symptoms of illness. The anti-psychotic medicines that she was now taking, different from the ones that had effectively worked for ten years, were not a good match for Krista.

When Krista went into a full blown psychotic episode and needed a treatment center, we didn't know where to take her, as the facility that had treated her earlier was now closed. A new center equidistant from our house came recommended to us and we managed, after much effort, to have Krista admitted there.

After seven days of treatment, the medical facility determined Krista was ready to be released. We were not convinced. We requested, to no avail, that Krista's antipsychotic prescription be changed back to the effective ones she had taken prior to her pregnancy. We knew Krista needed further treatment but had no choice when she was discharged. We took her home.

After two days at home, we were back to square one with a very ill Krista. Back to the treatment center we went. As any loving father would do, I became an advocate for her. I again pleaded with the medical staff to prescribe the antipsychotic medicine that had worked so well the past ten years. My pleadings were in vain. My frustrations with the staff reached a new level when a nurse told my daughter, while she was in full blown psychosis, that she could force me to leave by just asking. Since Krista thought I was someone only claiming to be her father, she asked the nurse to remove me and I was quickly escorted off the floor.

During this time, Katie had stepped out for a minute; when she came back she asked where I was. Krista replied, "he went bye-bye!" I certainly did go bye-bye, but this episode demonstrates the lack of understanding of Krista's illness and the frustrations that arise when family has little or no influence on a psychotic loved one's care.

Krista's husband, Clint, and I wrote the director of the facility, giving her the whole history of Krista's medicines and how they had worked so well for Krista pre-pregnancy, and they finally agreed to prescribe the anti-anxiety medication we requested. Krista began taking it again and soon improved. Our experience at this new facility was that they were good at treating drug and alcohol addictions, and also patients diagnosed with depression, but didn't seem to know how to treat people with bipolar disorder or schizophrenia. For Krista, this facility was the wrong place for her treatment.

Chapter 12

Bible Characters and Cigarettes

Krista Fliger

When I went to the "wrong place," I thought Jesus had returned and I was going to be in his special place. When I was checking in with my husband, parents, and uncle, I saw a tall worker in the hospital and thought he was Jesus. I would continue to think he was Jesus for the remainder of my stay. I thought other people were also Bible characters: David, Bathsheba and other wives of David, Jonathan, and Peter.

The facilities were new and nice at "the wrong place," but I still wanted out. My family came to visit me every day, but I couldn't see my son. Several

times a day, they let us out in the courtyard for a
smoke break. I don't smoke, except when I'm in a
mental hospital, apparently. It took me a long time
to learn to keep a cigarette lit, but I went outside
with the other smokers to socialize and feel the
fresh breeze. One day my mom jokingly said, "I
didn't know they smoked in heaven," and I replied "I
know, me neither!" She got a good laugh from that.
Who knows what heaven will be like but I suspect if
there is smoking, it will not be harmful to our
bodies.

Chapter 13

Unraveling

Krista

In the fall of 2019, I was realizing the medicine prescribed for me at the "wrong place" was not working for me. I felt suicidal, so I entered an intensive outpatient program rather than being readmitted. My mom babysat my son while I attended the outpatient program during the day.

A counselor in that program told me that everything has a reason, and that if I'm crying every day, I should try to figure out why. I decided to go back on the medicine I had been on before, even though it had not prevented a relapse. I started to unravel by Christmas while visiting my husband's family in

Florida. I thought my son was Jesus and had come back to earth as a baby.

When we got back to Ohio after our Florida visit, my parents came over during my son's naptime and they, along with my husband, tried to get me to go to the hospital. I was in a dark place and thought they were trying to do something against me. I thought they might be other people. Since I wouldn't go, they called the squad to come get me. I ran down to the basement when EMTs arrived, but eventually I was coaxed back upstairs. The EMTs were nice and treated me kindly, which I really appreciate in retrospect. My husband rode with me to the hospital.

At the hospital, my husband and mom waited with me to be admitted. I thought I had died and was waiting to go to heaven. I thought the other patients around me had also died and were waiting, too. I was finally admitted and spent the night in the emergency room, where I slept little. I had weird thoughts, imagining that some of the patients were robots. I thought I was being held captive by David's wives, so I knocked over a piece of furniture. When I did this, they put me in solitary confinement. I worried that I would never get out of there. By then, I was starting to think I was in hell rather than heaven. Finally, I was taken up to the mental health floor of the hospital where I was given a gown and escorted to my own room. The first patient I talked to said they had schizoaffective disorder, and I was excited to meet someone else who was going through similar things.

My time in the ward was scary; some of the patients around me had severe illnesses. I remember doing push ups whenever I felt I had messed up, a sign to me of my submission to God. My family came to see me often, which really helped me. This was in January 2020, right before COVID hit. Looking back, I am so glad I was there before COVID protocols stopped allowing visitors. Having my family around was vital to my recovery.

I ended up at this particular hospital because the doctor who had successfully treated me during my first psychotic episode nearly ten years before, and for some years after, was now working here. My father searched diligently until he found where my original doctor was now practicing. Once again, I was put under his care and he put me back on the medicine that helped me all those years prior to my

pregnancy.

Chapter 14

The Third Hospitalization

Katie

Growing up, I developed both a deep love and an immense respect for the ocean. I remember as a child being churned up in the surf like a t-shirt in a washing machine. I learned the best thing to do when a big wave is ready to crash down on you is to dive straight into it, counterintuitive as that may seem. When difficulties and sufferings arise, as they always will, my first impulse is to run the other way. While there may be times when flight is best, there are times to lean in, head-on, and fight.

Krista's third hospitalization came six months after the second hospitalization, and ten years after the first, almost to the day. During those months and years, there were other occasions when she was sick enough to be hospitalized, but we chose to care for her ourselves at home. I was available to do this during the day because of not having a job outside the home, a luxury many people do not have.

This time, Krista was not adequately medicated and her symptoms were worsening. She was still taking the drug she was on during pregnancy, but it was no longer working wonderfully as it had during that period. During her second hospitalization, she was simply prescribed higher doses of that same drug. Despite our pleas, the doctor she was seeing was reluctant to make a change. Something else needed to be done.

My husband did some research and found Krista's original doctor, who was now treating inpatients at a large local medical center and teaching at the associated university. We made the choice to take her there, even though no beds were available. In the 48 or so hours that she had to wait in the hospital's ER, her mental condition deteriorated significantly. Several times she refused to see me. When she did get a bed on the unit and I went to see her, she reacted with fear and distrust. I asked her who she thought I was. "A thief!" she shrieked. By now, it wasn't hard to recognize these behaviors as symptoms, and not take offense. I knew she was very sick.

Time and time again, I had seen the right medications work for Krista and trusted that they would again bring her back to health. We were relieved to have her under the care of her original physician, who remembered her and us, and put her back on her pre-pregnancy meds. I didn't know how long she would be hospitalized, but I knew it could take some time for her to recover.

I was now no longer afraid of "psych patients" as I had been ten years ago. Since we visited every day and Krista wasn't much into conversation at first, we found other people on the unit to talk to who were further along in their treatment and recovery. Many of them didn't have visitors. Beneath the jarring realities of mental illness, I began to see glimpses of caring and humanity, and it shrank the space between us.

I watched in wonder as a soft-spoken young man approached another male patient and told him to leave Krista alone. When Krista was finally discharged, I was deeply touched to witness a young woman give her what she had, literally the sweatshirt off her back, to take home to remember her by. Once again, I had found a beautiful community, one on a psychiatric unit, of all places.

Chapter 15

The Diagnosis

Katie

It was Sunday and traffic was light. Despite the chill and bleakness of January, I felt a warmth inside from having just been with our church community at our weekly worship service. I turned into the sprawling medical complex, glad to see the green letters "OPEN" at the parking garage nearest to my building. I parked, walked quickly, and presented myself at the reception desk.

By now, I knew the routine well. Place my driver's license and parking ticket (for validation) on the desk, state my name, patient's name and ID number. Then, walk to the lockers. I would always choose one from the same area, so that I would know where to return to get my things. Deposit coat, purse, and cell phone inside and shut the door. Enter a three-digit code. Again, always use the same one.

Up on the third floor, I called for a staff member, repeated the patient's name and ID number, and was escorted through two locked doors into the unit. My eyes quickly scanned the common area, looking for Krista. I was never quite sure what I would find, but after three weeks of treatment, her symptoms had improved quite a bit, so I was hopeful for a good visit. I signed in.

Visiting hours were much less restrictive at this facility. Normally Krista's husband, her dad, and I would each visit daily but at different times, but today I would be the only one coming since her husband had the flu and her dad was watching their son while I was gone. I spotted Krista sitting at a table and went to join her. She was quiet, unusually quiet.

Krista's doctor only came to the unit Monday through Friday, so I was very surprised when he appeared and sat down with us. We exchanged greetings, then he began to tell me that this morning while Krista was participating in a group activity, she caught a glimpse of a staff member's computer tablet. There was her name, and with it her diagnosis: schizophrenia.

In many ways this was not a surprise. A number of the symptoms were manifesting in ways we could clearly see. But still, it was a jolt. The word, with all its syllables, ricocheted in my mind. Her doctor was compassionate, and gently assured us that this did not change anything. However, the effect of the news on Krista was obvious, and I felt a deep sense of sadness and pain for her.

Throughout Krista's illness, I tried to keep three things in mind whenever we were in a difficult place: be calm, be kind, and be truthful. We had just heard a hard truth. I tried to be calm and kind. I would later wrestle with the diagnosis, with its pop culture images and societal stigmas. I would later ask the "whys," and wonder again if I could've somehow protected my precious baby from what was happening. But for now, I only wanted to do everything I could to help her through. I can't remember exactly what we talked about or what we did. I do remember that I stayed much longer than I had expected, and wasn't able to text or call home with a reason. I would have to find a delicate way to break the news to the rest.

Chapter 16

A Lucky One

Krista

When I first saw the diagnosis of schizophrenia on the tablet next to my name, I knew it was more serious than schizoaffective disorder, or bipolar I. Somehow, seeing the word made me feel more disabled. Coming out of the hospital, I think knowing the diagnosis hindered my recovery. Perhaps it was merely age or some other factor, but the year following that hospitalization was difficult and fraught with setbacks.

I went to an outpatient clinic recommended by my doctor and found a good nurse practitioner, who I'll call Eric. Eric kept me on the medicine that had successfully worked for me. I feel fortunate to have a medicine that works for me. I think it's part of God's provision in my life.

I went about being a mother to my son. I placed him in preschool two days a week, primarily for him to get the social interaction and learning that children need, but also for me to get the rest and self-care I needed. It also allowed me to get things done around the house. When you have a condition like schizophrenia, you have to know your limits and not exceed them as my doctor constantly reminds me.

A friend once said that I am one of the lucky ones with schizophrenia because I do so well. That made me feel good. Another friend said she saw the positive impact medicine made in my life, and it inspired her to try medicine to help with her depression. Our stories have power to make positive change, so I remind myself to not be afraid to tell mine. I have schizophrenia, but I am still the same girl, now woman, that I have always been.

Chapter 17

What Has Helped Me

Krista

I have learned a few things during my experiences that I want to pass along to anyone struggling with their mental health. First, work closely with your doctor or nurse practitioner. Have your spouse or trusted friend or family member come along with you to appointments. Listen to what your medical professionals say, and follow their guidance while still allowing for your own judgment.

Go to counseling. Don't feel like you have to go to the same counselor forever. At times, I needed one counselor and at other times a different therapist was vital in moving me forward. I have found much healing in counseling sessions.

Do not mask your feelings, but talk about them, experience them, and then change your thinking about situations to nudge your feelings to more positive ones. This is the most important lesson I learned about in graduate school, I think. Look into Cognitive Behavioral Theory for more information on that.

Learn as much as you can about mental health and healing. Educate yourself online. Take a class. The more you know, the better you will be able to help yourself.

Be sure to exercise regularly. Taking a yoga class at my local gym proved valuable to me when I wasn't feeling well. Yoga emphasizes breathwork and meditation, which many therapists also recommend. Exercising increases endorphins which are good for the mind and body. Being physically active can help reduce depression. Today, I do yoga at the yoga studio in my city.

Find a support system. Mine are my spouse, parents, family, friends, and church. Your support system may differ, but be sure you have one. Finding a mental health support group is also beneficial.

Know your limits. Don't put too much on your plate when you're struggling with mental illness. For me, stress is a trigger so I have to be aware of how much I can handle and be mindful to avoid too much stress. This was hard for me as I always planned on having two kids, but my husband and I decided it would be too stressful for me to have a second child. Being mindful of my limits, I've also chosen to wait to return to work as a counselor rather than pushing my limits.

My faith in Jesus Christ has been the number one factor in my healing as far as I'm concerned! If you don't know him as your personal Savior, I invite you to open your heart to him today. The Bible says "For God so loved the world that he gave his one and only Son, so that whoever believes in him shall not perish but have everlasting life." He can make beauty from ashes and uses all of our brokenness for good, if we let him. Others may prefer following a higher power or their own conscience. Having someone or something to focus on can be a great

help to healing.

Chapter 18

NIMH Study

Ivan

Several years ago, Krista, Katie, and I agreed to
participate in a study from the National Institute of
Mental Health (NIMH), enlisting people with
Mennonite and Amish backgrounds who have a
connection with bipolar disorder. The Mennonite
sect started in Europe, but in the mid-1600's,
religious persecution forced many Mennonites to
flee to North America, where they often formed
tight-knit communities. Living in such groups led to
a relatively small gene pool among Mennonites and
Amish, making them more vulnerable to certain
genetic markers and a valuable group for genetic

studies. Bipolar disorder is known to have a genetic factor of around 75%. It certainly gives us pause to know our DNA most likely contributed to Krista's illness.

While Krista was later diagnosed with schizophrenia, bipolar is closely related. "We find that very often, the same genes express themselves in different ways among relatives, so some people who carry the gene might have a severe form of bipolar disorder, some might have another illness such as depression or anxiety, and others might be perfectly fine," says Dr. McMahon of NIMH.

We were happy to participate in the NIMH study; it gives us joy to contribute any way we can to understanding the causes and treatments of mental illness. We long for new and improved medicines to better control symptoms and even, hopefully, for an eventual cure.

Chapter 19

What I've Learned

Katie

It was Krista's idea to write a book. These are our words. These are our stories.

Thirteen years have passed since Krista's first hospitalization. It's been a journey both beautiful and awful. It's taken me through the wilderness and up to high vistas. These experiences have taught me and changed me.

Krista's first episode of psychosis was a shock. It was unfamiliar and completely unexpected. At the time, I was just hoping to find a way through it. As weeks and months passed, I tried to understand everything in an attempt to bring some control over the situation. Eventually, I came to realize there are things I have no power over and questions that will remain unanswerable, and I can be okay with that.

Krista's doctor encouraged her to do two things: to plan well and to know her limits, wise advice for anyone. Planning well is a matter of intention, but to truly find our limits we must first burn through all of our abilities and resources, and that can be terrifying. It can also be the genesis of something new and wonderful.

My experiences over the past thirteen years have changed me. I have seen roots of faith, hope and love grow deeper. I am learning, albeit slowly at times, to live differently, to be more curious, to be quicker to listen, and slower to judge. Rather than running away in fear, I may now choose to tackle difficult obstacles head-on. I am learning to let go of things that are beyond my control.

During the most difficult times, I find hope in the enduring power of love. Krista is, and has always been, one of the most loving people I have ever known. She has an amazing spouse who has remained steadfastly by her side, his unruffled presence bringing stability in the midst of chaos. Together they have a beautiful, healthy child who lights up all of our lives.

Nevertheless, struggles persist. Such is the nature of living with chronic illness. To varying degrees, such is the nature of life for all of us, because suffering, and not only joy, is part of what it means to be human. Life is not perfect nor predictable. We need each other to navigate through and adapt to life's inevitable changes.

This is not a book of answers, it is one family's experience. I hope that by sharing our story we can increase understanding in the area of mental health. I hope we can help bring down barriers that divide people and eliminate labels that unfairly judge people. I hope that we can, in some small way, help the world become a more loving place.

Chapter 20

It Takes All of Us

Ivan

Each person affected by mental illness responds to treatment in their own way. Krista's medicines have changed and doses have been adjusted over the years. What may have worked at one point may need to be changed later. Determining the best medicines and dosages for a patient can take years of trial and error. Since doctors, nurse practitioners, and nurses do not see the day-to-day life of a patient, input from the patient and family is necessary. During stressful times, doses may need to be adjusted accordingly.

Krista, along with our family, began supporting NAMI (National Alliance on Mental Illness) by participating in the annual fundraiser of our local affiliate. NAMI offers a tremendous number of resources for those seeking information and help throughout the country. In some parts of the world, neither support nor resources are available. My heart goes out to families struggling with mental health issues, especially in areas with few helpful resources.

For me, knowing that the loving, kind and empathetic daughter I know is still there, even when illness overwhelms her brain, and that those attributes will return once her brain chemistry returns to more normal levels, is something I have had to learn. A diabetic needs insulin to return to normal function when sugar levels are off. In the same way, a schizophrenic needs a chemically-balanced brain. Unfortunately, brain chemistry does not always balance quickly even with proper medication, so the process from unstable to normal function can take far longer than we like. While my wife is a patient person, I am not. I've had to learn to surrender my impatience and frustration and realize some things are out of my control. I am still a work in progress in this regard! Our family has rallied around Krista's mental health care and we all contribute as we best know how. Sometimes we make mistakes or get impatient, but I believe Krista, when well, has always felt loved and supported.

For me, it has been a somewhat similar pathway through the psychological progression one goes through during grief, as explained by Elisabeth Kubler-Ross in her book *On Death and Dying*. I definitely began with denial, thinking Krista's breakdown was a one-time event. Recurrence moved me beyond denial and into anger. Why did this have to happen? Who has control of this? Krista certainly did not deserve this, nor make choices that could've led to her illness. I was often and at times still am angry.

As a father, I've often wished I could take on the disease for Krista, freeing her from the difficult symptoms she experiences. I suppose this is my bargaining stage. I've also dipped my toes in and out of the depression stage. I find that being grateful for all the wonderful things in life, notably family and friends, helps me through grief and depression. Seeing how Krista handles all that her disease requires of her is also motivating for me.

For me, acceptance involves being at peace with mental illness and how it affects people. Mental illness, in many different forms, is part of life for most people. Being at peace with mental illness allows me to more easily flow with the crazy up and down swings common for many. Surrendering does not mean giving in to the disease, but rather trying to understand it and learning how to best manage it.

Awareness of mental health in our country is increasing, but we as a society still have a long way to go to overcome the stigma associated with mental illnesses. In a February 9, 2023 opinion piece by Ann O'Donnell, the Ohio governor's chief advisor and printed in "The Columbus Dispatch," O'Donnell writes: "Mental illness is not a character defect. It's not about willpower or just talking and staying on your meds. It's a disease of the brain, one that can be devastating if ignored and untreated. I am writing this to tell the world that my mother had a brain disorder. She was sick. Her mental illness was as much a disease as cancer, diabetes, or arthritis." O'Donnell explains that, after years of struggling with mental illness, her mother came to terms with it and accepted it without a complaint. She concludes the piece with "No--my mother wasn't like the other mothers. She was extraordinary." Krista isn't like other daughters. She

is extraordinary. Today is a day of Hope!

Chapter 21

This Present Moment

Krista

Scientists, counselors, and psychiatrists are working on a better day for patients with mental health disorders. We are making progress on eliminating stigmas and finding effective treatments, but much hard work remains. Still, today is a day of hope.

My dad got our family involved in raising money every year with an organization named NAMI, the National Alliance on Mental Illness. Every year, NAMI organizes walks around the country to raise money to help those affected by mental illness. This is one way we give back and work toward hope for those with mental illness and their families.

My life would likely be much different had I experienced my disease during a different time in history. Our understanding of the brain and the disorders that can arise from unbalanced brain chemistry is vastly superior to those of the past. The medicines and treatments we use today are also much more effective. We have made great strides in treating mental illnesses; I eagerly anticipate that further gains will continue to improve mental health outcomes.

On a different note, hardly anyone argues that it's fair when an illness happens. Is it fair that I can't have a second child because pregnancy, delivery, and postpartum could put the baby and me at risk?

Is it fair that I can't be a counselor right now because I'm not well enough according to my husband and parents? No, in my opinion it's not fair. So what do I do with this? Again, I turn to my faith in God for answers. John 12:25 tells us, "Whoever loves his life will lose it, while whoever hates his life in this world will keep it for eternal life."

Years ago on a mission trip, I surrendered my life. I said, "God, you can do whatever you want with my life, but use it to advance your kingdom, glorify you, and help others." This is the way he decided to work, so I must be okay with it. Helping others who are going through similar dark experiences with mental illness gives me purpose. Mental illness need not define you. Keep going and never give up. Today is a day of hope!

I have learned to kind of separate myself from my diagnosis. I have an illness, but my illness does not define me. At times, I feel sad knowing that I am part of the one percent of the US population that develops schizophrenia. Knowing what I go through makes me want to help others who struggle with mental illness in whatever way I can. If I can help one person with my story, then it will be worth it.

Today, I'm grateful for my faith, marriage, son, family, friends and more. I'm grateful to live in a time when there is medicine that works and professionals who care. And I am forever grateful for my support network of friends and family who help me on my journey. One of my goals is to stay out of the hospital forever. Another is to get back to working, perhaps when my son goes to school.

One aspect of my illness is I often focus on heaven and the future instead of just being present and in the moment. If I don't watch myself, it can threaten to steal joy from the moment. Focusing on each day rather than looking ahead helps me listen to God's still, small voice today, rather than worry about the future. Jesus tells us in his Gospels not to worry about tomorrow. He knows our frailty and loves us anyway. He has provided for me my whole life, so why would he stop now?

I wrote this book to be an encouragement and perhaps a beacon of light to anyone struggling with mental illness. Having mental illness is not your fault. Just like any other part of the body can get sick or diseased, so can the brain and the way the neurotransmitters fire. So take courage, take hope, and advocate for others who are going through similar things. God can use your experiences to touch other lives for the better.

I have found peace and joy from friends and family. The doctor encouraging me during my first hospitalization was correct; even with everything I went though, I earned both my bachelor and master degrees, met my husband and soulmate, and have a family. I have creative work and hobbies to keep me going. I have a wonderful life and I thank God for this blessing.

Thanks for reading our stories. Make sure you understand and tell others your story. If you struggle with mental illness, keep working toward your goals and never give up. I hope our stories help you find your hope, that even with the most disturbing diagnoses to your soul, you can with God's help live a fulfilled life with full relationships, jobs, and hobbies. Never give up that hope, stay in the present, and let God heal you. You may be surprised at what God has in store.

Giving back and moving forward…

10% of revenue from this book will go directly to the National Alliance on Mental Illness and other organizations fighting stigma and helping people get better access to mental health treatment. Thanks for making a difference in the lives of those in need of help to gain mental health! YOU can make a difference and you are.

Made in the USA
Monee, IL
11 December 2023

48865297R00069